# Headline Series

OCT 1 0 1984

No. 268    FOREIGN POLICY ASSOCIATION    $3.00

# THE ATLANTIC ALLIANCE AT 35

by A. W. DePorte

Foreword by Alexander M. Haig Jr. ...... 3

**1**  The Balance Sheet ..................................... 7

**2**  The Security of the
      North Atlantic Area .............................. 15

**3**  Grand Strategy? ....................................... 30

**4**  The Third World ...................................... 39

**5**  Economic Relations ................................. 48

**6**  The Future ............................................... 55

*Talking It Over* ...................................... 62
*Reading List* .......................................... 63

Cover Design: Hersch Wartik        March/April 1984

## The Author

A. W. DEPORTE was a career official of the U.S. Department of State for 25 years, where he served as a member of the policy planning staff and as director of the office of research on Western Europe. He is now a visiting scholar at the Institute of French Studies, New York University. He holds a doctorate in international relations from the University of Chicago. Dr. DePorte is the author of *De Gaulle's Foreign Policy, 1944–1946* (Cambridge, Mass., Harvard University Press, 1968) and *Europe Between the Superpowers: The Enduring Balance* (New Haven, Conn., Yale University Press, 1979).

## The Foreign Policy Association

The Foreign Policy Association is a private, nonprofit, nonpartisan educational organization. Its purpose is to stimulate wider interest and more effective participation in, and greater understanding of, world affairs among American citizens. Among its activities is the continuous publication, dating from 1935, of the HEADLINE SERIES. The authors are responsible for factual accuracy and for the views expressed. FPA itself takes no position on issues of United States foreign policy.

### Editorial Advisory Committee
*Chairman:* Stanley H. Hoffmann

*Members*
Carol Edler Baumann
Earl W. Foell
John Lewis Gaddis
Edwin Newman
Ponchitta Pierce

Eleanor Singer
Andrew F. Smith
James A. Van Fleet
Samuel S. Vaughan
Leo M. Weins
Allen Weinstein

HEADLINE SERIES (ISSN 0017-8780) is published five times a year, January, March, May, September and November, by the Foreign Policy Association, Inc., 205 Lexington Ave., New York, N.Y. 10016. Chairman, Leonard H. Marks; President, Archie E. Albright; Editor, Nancy L. Hoepli; Associate Editors, Ann R. Monjo and Mary E. Stavrou. Subscription rates, $12.00 for 5 issues; $20.00 for 10 issues; $28.00 for 15 issues. Single copy price $3.00. Discount 25% on 10 to 99 copies; 30% on 100 to 499; 35% on 500 to 999; 40% on 1,000 or more. Payment must accompany order for $6 or less. Second-class postage paid at New York, N.Y. POSTMASTER: Send address changes to HEADLINE SERIES, Foreign Policy Association, 205 Lexington Ave., New York, N.Y. 10016. Copyright 1984 by Foreign Policy Association, Inc. Composed and printed at Science Press, Ephrata, Pa.

Library of Congress Catalog No. 84-81644
ISBN 0-87124-091-2

# Foreword

## by Alexander M. Haig Jr.

Anniversaries are usually the time for stocktaking, among individuals and nations. By the standards of most of its member nations, NATO, at 35 years of age, is an infant; by the standards of the individual, a young adult; by the standards of alliances, an incredibly long-lived elder. Depending upon one's perspective, it is easy to judge the alliance on its birthday as an uncoordinated baby, a still-gangling youth or a remarkably spry but aged gerontocrat.

A. W. DePorte has an excellent feel for these differing perspectives, the expectations they arouse, and the achievements and disappointments inspired by NATO performance. With his keen analytic grasp of the issues leavened by a sense of history, DePorte has done an excellent job of depicting the alliance from its formation period to the current day. Finding the "floor" of the alliance in a still-shared fear of the Soviet Union, he probes the "ceiling"—the extent to which the alliance can find common ground on the perennial issues of military doctrine, burden-sharing, global strategy and international economics.

The alliance is not a government, its members are not united in all spheres by a common interest, and not all problems can be resolved by the alliance approach, even if those problems affect its performance in the security field. Still, the issues can be "worked," as diplomats are fond of saying, and the crucial task of providing security against the Soviet threat can be performed, so long as the allies—above all the United States—keep their eyes on NATO's basic function. Perhaps the key concept is balance—a sense of proportion in keeping disagreements on other issues from crippling the NATO deterrent.

---

Alexander M. Haig Jr., former Secretary of State (1981–82), served as Supreme Allied Commander of NATO forces in Europe from 1974 to 1979.

DePorte observes that the founders of the alliance, those "present at the creation" (to use Secretary of State Dean Acheson's phrase), thought that NATO was that best of all devices, a temporary expedient to achieve a permanent result. They believed that a secure West might bring about the retrenchment and mellowing of the East. Ironically, these men, famous for farsighted statesmanship, planned only for the near term. Ever since, alliance diplomacy has been characterized by creative activity, born of crisis conditions, that somehow outlasted the crisis to become a permanent, constructive part of the alliance's security. Hence, NATO's paradoxical reputation: the focus of a huge industry of critics (the only industry in the West unaffected by the economic cycle), yet somehow an enduring testimony to the capacity of free nations to cooperate effectively for the common good.

We must beware of falling into one of two extremes when we look at NATO. The alliance is not in such bad shape that it hardly functions except to drain its members of precious resources and to frustrate creative diplomacy. But the alliance is not in such good shape that its success can be taken for granted and its achievements regarded as eternal. To make NATO work for us, we must work for it.

To work for NATO now means to me to take action on three increasingly interrelated issues: first, to make basic alliance strategy more credible; second, to improve our approach to common economic problems, recognizing that the guns-versus-butter argument can only be resolved through greater economic growth; third, to find ways to work together on issues that affect NATO security even though they do not fall within NATO's technical boundaries. In short, the members of NATO should try to raise the ceiling of their cooperation. If they do not, then the floor of their security itself may be weakened.

Much of the recent debate over alliance strategy has been influenced by our somewhat tardy response to a steady and relentless Soviet military buildup in both the nuclear and conventional areas. We are all well aware of the balanced approach symbolized by the two-track decision of 1979 to modernize intermediate nuclear forces and, at the same time, try to make them superfluous through negotiations. It is perhaps a measure of how some in the West like to denigrate NATO's achievements that the successful deployment of the new missiles, despite unprecedented Soviet attempts to prevent it, has in itself become a matter for recrimination. In the wake of the success in implementing the 1979 decision, NATO's deterrence has been strengthened, but this is not enough. It is surely not sensible to declare NATO's strategy obsolete or inherently defective at the very moment when we have taken a major step to sustain it. Clearly, the conventional forces must also be improved. In an era when Western public opinion has been aroused once more by fears of nuclear war, we should be doing ourselves a disservice if we were to enlarge the nuclear engagement through neglect of our conventional forces. To put it simply: the strategy is sound if the resources are provided, and if the resources are not provided, no strategy can succeed, least of all one that further degrades the universal need for a sound deterrent—a credible Western level at every level of Soviet threat.

That brings up the second issue—the conflict between guns and butter. The United States and its allies have experienced a series of economic reversals over the last decade that cumulatively have raised practical and philosophical questions about the welfare state as we have known it. Carefully wrought political and industrial compromises that worked well for three decades have been undone. In every member of the alliance, major political parties have renewed the search for a new social contract. The coincidence of these disturbances with the need to meet Soviet military expansion has created major challenges.

The solution is not to pretend that we face a mutually exclusive choice of guns or butter. Domestic reform can be pursued only in the context of national security. National security in turn depends upon domestic consensus. We must succeed at doing both or we shall surely fail to do either.

In 1984, this means a fresh resolve to avoid the dangers of protectionism. It means a renewal of the constructive forces of European unity. It means a long overdue American initiative to deal with budget deficits and high interest rates. Surely, the leaders of NATO, in cooperation with Japan, can work to rejuvenate economic growth, which will ease the always difficult task of providing the resources for deterrence and defense.

Third and finally, NATO members have begun to recognize that the Soviet Union has become a power with global military reach. We cannot expect NATO to create its own global strategy, nor should we expect all members of NATO to share the same perspective on Soviet actions in the third world. Yet almost unnoticed, those members of NATO best able to handle challenges beyond NATO's formal sphere have tried to meet them together. In the Sinai multinational forces, they succeeded; in the Beirut multinational forces, they failed; in the Persian Gulf, the verdict is still out. At the very least, these experiences teach us that consistent leadership by the United States, frequent consultation and mutual understanding of the interests at stake are the fundamental ingredients of success.

Sometime in the nature of living things there must be growth or there will be decay. The seemingly solid institutions of today, if not adapted to changing circumstances, will wither before the eyes of our children tomorrow. NATO at 35 has an impressive history of mastering both challenge and change. The foundation is there; the resources are there; those who cherish freedom and democracy support it. The Atlantic alliance has survived less on the merit of tidy conceptual schemes than on the ingenuity of its diplomats, the courage of its leaders, and the resolve of its peoples. As we celebrate its achievements, we should draw upon these assets so that the NATO of the future can be as much a master of its destiny as the NATO of the past.

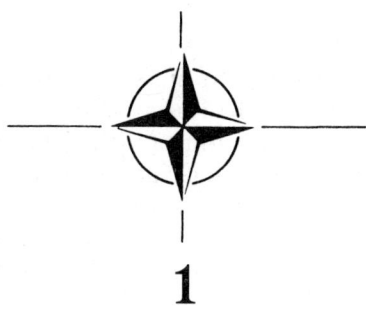

# 1

# The Balance Sheet

On April 4, 1949, the leaders of 12 nations gathered in Washington to sign the North Atlantic treaty. According to Article 5, its central provision,

> [The parties] agree that an armed attack against one or more of them ... shall be considered an attack against them all, and consequently agree that, if such an armed attack occurs, each of them, in exercise of the right of individual or collective self-defense ... will assist the party or parties so attacked by taking forthwith, individually and in concert with the other parties, such action as it deems necessary, including the use of armed force.

This commitment did not mean that any party would go to war automatically if another was attacked. Each would act as it thought "necessary" in the circumstances on the basis of its own constitutional procedures. The treaty could not have been approved in the United States had this been otherwise. But it was clear nonetheless that the United States, for the first time in its history, was departing from President George Washington's hallowed counsel against alliances "with any portion of the foreign world" to make a formal commitment to act in the future as if an attack on any of a group of foreign countries was an attack on itself. In principle the 10 European signatories and Canada were making the same commitment to the United States and each other. In practice they were placing themselves behind the shield of American power in order to deter, and if necessary defeat, an attack by the Soviet Union on their territories as well as to prevent intimidating Soviet pressure on their freedom of action and internal stability.

Few of the signatories would have predicted in 1949 that the treaty would still be in force 35 years later and that the alliance would still include the 12 original members (the United States, Canada, the United Kingdom, France, Belgium, the Netherlands, Luxembourg, Denmark, Norway, Iceland, Portugal and Italy) and four others (Greece and Turkey became members in 1952, the Federal Republic of Germany, or FRG, in 1955 and Spain in 1982). Fewer would have imagined that the basic premises of the alliance would remain unchanged over so many years: the common awareness of a Soviet threat to the interests of all and a common belief that that threat could be met at least risk and cost by means of a formal security tie between the United States and the countries of Western Europe.

### *American Guarantee*

The founders of the alliance did not think that they were building what would become a "permanent" security system. On the contrary, they thought that they were providing an answer to a more or less short-term problem. The Soviet Union, as they saw it, had emerged from World War II as overwhelmingly the strongest power in Europe. It had absorbed Eastern Europe, including part of Germany, into its sphere of influence by force and seemed able to absorb some or all of Western Europe, including the remainder of Germany. The devastated countries of Western Europe could not then deter or repel a Soviet attack. Economically weak and politically divided, they were prey to Soviet intimidation or subversion (two of them—France and Italy—contained powerful Communist parties). They could be made secure against these threats—and given time and confidence

■ NATO Countries (excluding N.A.)

▥ Warsaw Pact Countries

© 1982 by The New York Times Company, Reprinted by permission.

to rebuild their societies and defenses—only by an American guarantee, together with American aid. But it was believed that this state of things was essentially temporary, for two reasons.

▶The U.S. policy of containment, of which the Atlantic alliance was a part, was based on the belief that Soviet expansionism was rooted in the nature of the Communist regime. George F. Kennan's classic statement of American postwar policy in the July 1947 issue of *Foreign Affairs* (under the signature of "X") had argued that if the Soviet Union could be prevented from expanding into the areas of weakness around it, and particularly

Western Europe, its regime would eventually mellow and its expansionist drive wither away. The alliance then would become superfluous.
▶The countries of Western Europe were likely to recover their normal economic strength and political and social stability even before such changes took place in the Soviet Union. They then would be able to provide for their own security in the face of Soviet threats of attack, intimidation or subversion. Something like the classical European balance-of-power system would be restored. The United States could then take a much less direct interest in the affairs of the old Continent.

There were some even in 1949 who argued that these premises of the alliance were faulty. The noted American journalist and author Walter Lippmann, among others, believed that Soviet foreign policy derived at least as much from the historic expansionism personified by Czar Peter I and Empress Catherine II as from the doctrines of Marx and Lenin. This view had implications for policy which were both less and more encouraging than those of the official position. On the one hand, the Russian tendency to expand into areas of weakness, and particularly into the adjacent areas of Eastern and Central Europe which Russia had controlled or coveted for centuries, was not likely to disappear or mellow even if contained or even if the Soviet regime itself somehow became less Communist. In other words, the problem of Russian power casting its shadow over Western Europe (as well as other areas) would last as long as a powerful Russian state lasted, under whatever system of government. At the same time, Soviet policy, according to this view, was more likely to be expressed by traditional methods of pressure and influence-building than by the kind of ideologically inspired propensity to use force which some thought Bolshevik Russia shared with Nazi Germany. If so, there might even be possibilities for negotiation with the U.S.S.R. on specific subjects.

Some critics also doubted that the countries of Western Europe, even if they rebuilt their economies and societies, would be able to deal with the Soviet Union as more or less equal members of a restored European balance-of-power system. The Soviet Union, though severely hurt by World War II, could (together with its satellite states in Eastern Europe) tap human and military resources on a level which the nation-states of Western Europe, even fully restored, would not be able to match. These countries would have to unite their defense efforts if they were to have any chance of striking a balance with the U.S.S.R. without American help. This was unimaginable in 1949, and little progress has been made toward it since.

The premises underlying the creation of the alliance in 1949 implied that its success would be measured by its ability to contribute to conditions which would allow it to disappear in time. A successful alliance, by these standards, would have been one that vanished long ago. The fact that the alliance still exists after 35 years would seem to be a proof, by this measure, of its lack of success. The Soviet threat, even though contained in Europe, has not disappeared, nor have the European allies achieved a capability of dealing with it unaided by the United States.

But this paradox is more apparent than real. The founders of the alliance may have erred in some of their expectations, but their most basic purpose, after all, was to assure the security of Western Europe against Soviet attack, intimidation or subversion and, by doing that, to protect American interests in the survival of a Western Europe so secured. This objective has been so well achieved over 35 years that the success has long since been taken for granted and, therefore, often overlooked.

In addition, the alliance which was created in 1949 to deal with a given set of circumstances has produced benefits which could have been imagined only dimly at the start, if at all.

● World War II was not ended by a peace treaty, yet Europe was stabilized as a result of the cold war itself, for better *and* worse, in a way which no treaty might have accomplished. The alliance of Western nations, including the United States, is a central component of that stability, as is the bloc (known as the Warsaw Pact) held together by Soviet coercion in Eastern Europe. Together they form a new European international system which has replaced the one that broke down irreparably in

World War II. It is easy to imagine systems that might be better (involving, for example, the independence of Eastern Europe) or worse (involving Soviet domination of Western Europe or a Germany pursuing reunification by force or threat). But the system we have was achieved without war and has been maintained because it divides least those with the power to change it.

• The Western alliance has also come to be seen as the most visible expression of a broader community of interests among the United States, Canada and Western Europe, which includes economic and cultural as well as security and political ties. The alliance has been widely understood to be more than an old-style military pact. But disagreements about just what "more" means have created difficulties of overexpectation that will be discussed.

• The alliance has been particularly important with respect to the "German problem," on which the victors of World War II could reach no explicit agreement. The FRG was created by the three Western powers out of their zones of occupation and armed as a part of their cold-war struggle with the Soviet Union. Many at the time feared that a new West German state might play an independent and dangerous role in European affairs in pursuit of reunification or even recovery of the German territory lost to Poland and the U.S.S.R. This concern has turned out to be groundless. The FRG has kept reunification as a national goal. But, whatever hopes it had in the early 1950s that Western "situations of strength" would eventually force or induce the Soviet Union to allow reunification, it has never tried to attain that objective by way of negotiations with the Russians and neutralization. It has always considered the security tie with the United States its highest priority. In addition, the FRG's membership in the alliance and in the European institutions that have grown up alongside it has symbolized the FRG's integration into the postwar democratic system of the West.

West German membership also has strengthened the alliance, and not only militarily. After the Korean War began in June 1950, the United States decided that the FRG would have to contribute to its own defense and to that of Western Europe. But France and its other neighbors, with memories of World War II still so sharp, refused to accept the FRG's rearmament without guarantees. One such guarantee was the creation at this time of the Western European Union (WEU), established by France, Britain, Italy, Belgium, the Netherlands and Luxembourg, as well as the FRG, to ensure that West German armament remained within prescribed limits. But the WEU has never been of much importance. The real guarantee of the FRG's correct behavior, from the point of view of its neighbors, has always been the fact that its armed forces are fully integrated into a system dominated by the United States, that is, the Atlantic alliance. What was true in 1954–55 still remains true. A militarily powerful FRG, cut loose from the tactfully managed alliance ties that restrain as well as protect it, would be seen by many as a disturbing element in the international relations of Europe. The fact that the West Germans consistently have put security ahead of reunification and muted their policy and power within the alliance system has much enhanced the latter's value for the Europeans.

*A Voluntary Association*

The alliance has survived the failure of some of its original expectations. It also has survived the many immense changes which have transformed the devastated Europe of 1945. But one important thing has not changed: the fact that each member country continues to find the alliance important to its own well-being.

The Atlantic alliance is not a state or government. It has no independent existence. It is a voluntary association by means of which the member countries take care of some (not all) of their national interests. It can survive and function only for as long as they believe that it provides the best available (not necessarily the best imaginable) means to secure those particular interests at acceptable cost and risk. The alliance is "recreated" every day, or at least every time there is a change of leadership in a member country or a significant change in the international environment. It remains alive in 1984 because the American, British, French, West German and 12 other governments choose to keep it alive, each for reasons of its own. President Ronald Reagan, British Prime Minister Margaret Thatcher, French President François Mitterrand, West German Chancellor Helmut Kohl and the other government leaders find the alliance useful for their needs just as their many predecessors had done. Foreign policy is only one of the issues that affect the outcome of elections in these democratic countries. But it is fair to assume that a majority of voters (if not all the citizens all the time) have found their governments' policies with respect to the alliance acceptable or tolerable as compared to alternatives that might be feasible.

It is a remarkable fact, however, that there has almost never been a moment in the long life of the alliance when its officials or outside observers have been completely satisfied with its performance. One reason for this is that international circumstances change rapidly, and the alliance members are constantly challenged to keep the institution abreast of these changes. A second reason, as suggested above, is that the alliance is perceived to be more than a classical military pact, yet there never has been a full meeting of minds among the members about just what more it is. The fact that it is the visible expression of a wider community raises expectations of more far-reaching agreement than a realistic consideration of the very diverse locations, outlooks and interests of the members would suggest is possible. The fact that the members think of themselves not only as allies in cold blood but as friends and even "cousins" makes their inevitable disagreements about alliance business as well as other things seem somehow more unacceptable than would otherwise be the case.

It is a safe guess that this pattern of strength and division, success and failure, will continue in the future. Recognizing that fact helps us match our expectations to reality and thus helps ensure the survival of the alliance for as long as it serves some of the important interests of the members. For that reason it is useful to examine both the possibilities and the potential limitations of common action among the allies in each of the major areas in which their policies interact: security, relations with the U.S.S.R., the world outside Europe, and international economic issues.

## 2

# The Security of the North Atlantic Area

For the United States the Soviet threat is worldwide. It takes many forms, of which direct military aggression is only one, and it calls for many kinds of response. Confrontations in one area are seen as affecting those in others. For Americans, Western Europe is one theater of a broader conflict, important in itself but not necessarily more important at all times than other areas.

For the European allies, on the other hand, their Continent is not a theater but is home. The security of their countries is their highest priority. They know that this is not the case for the United States on whom, however, their security depends. There are also different perceptions of the Soviet threat among them, different degrees of the feeling of insecurity. Some of them directly face the Soviet Union or its allies; some are placed behind those that do; Britain still has a traditional sense of relative insular security; France believes that its national nuclear force makes it more secure than its neighbors; Spain and Portugal have little feeling of direct involvement in affairs north of the Pyrenees; Greece and Turkey are preoccupied with each other. These countries do not all perceive the Soviet Union in the same way.

Even so, most of them have a sense of the dangers of having to live permanently next to, or near, a totalitarian superpower of whose intentions they can never be sure. Few in Western Europe have feared Soviet attack since the Korean War, or at least since the Cuban missile crisis of 1962. But the Europeans have a constant sense of permanent threat which neither declined much during the springtime of détente in the early 1970s nor increased much when the Soviet Union invaded such a distant country as Afghanistan. Few in Europe thought that the prospects of a Soviet march westward had been increased by that invasion. The United States saw the invasion very differently. Such differences have been the source of important tension in the alliance when the United States wanted the reluctant European allies to increase their armament or take other measures in response to some Soviet action elsewhere which it, but not they, thought affected adversely the security of Western Europe.

The difficulties which these differences of perception cause in the alliance are reinforced by the fact that there is such a diversity of means of military action among the members. One is a global nuclear superpower; two others have national nuclear forces; these three and one or two others have significant conventional forces; most of the others have only small or ill-armed forces or, in the case of Iceland, none. These differences make it difficult for many of the allies to think that their contributions to the common defense—whether a little more or a little less—count for much. They also make it hard for their leaders and people even to remain conversant with the increasingly complex issues of strategic policymaking on which they know their well-being depends. In addition, there is not one ally, including even the most powerful, whose ability to spend money on what the alliance says is needed for defense is immune to competing domestic political pressures for the allocation of its resources.

## *Keeping Pace with Technology*

All these sources of discord might have become of marginal importance to the alliance by this time if its strategy and supporting arrangements could have been decided upon once and

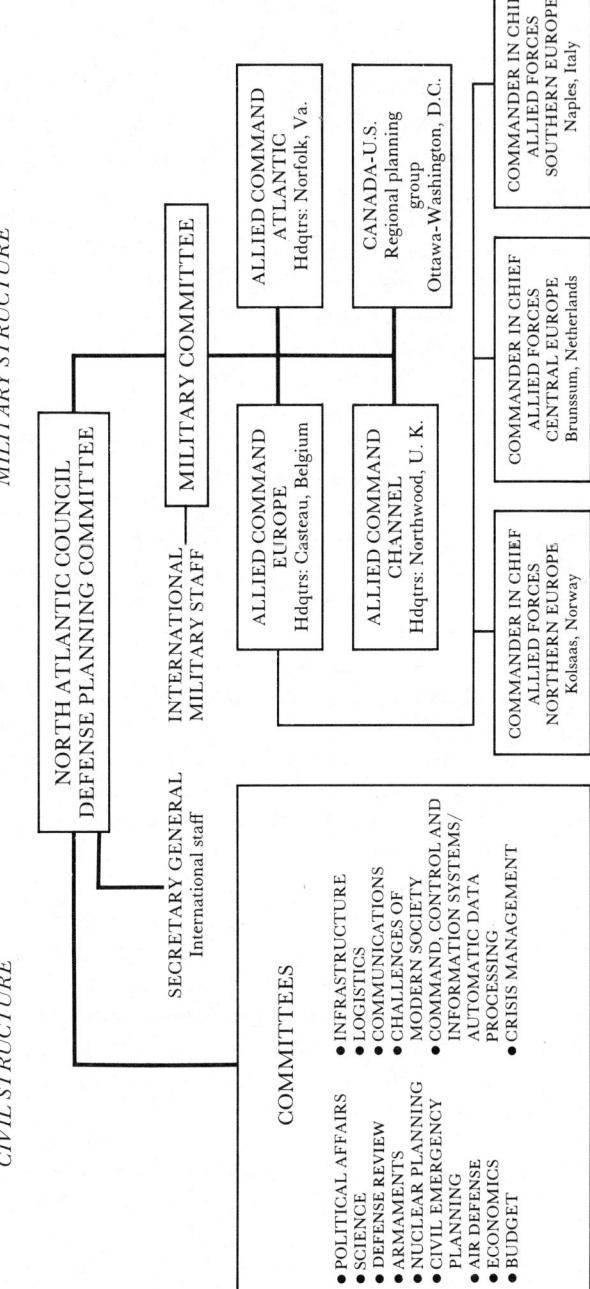

for all and put in place. But the march of military technology makes that impossible. No sooner do the allies reach an understanding of what needs to be done, and proceed (with whatever difficulties) to try to do it, than new weapons come along which undermine the credibility of the existing plans. The process then has to be repeated. The ensuing debate brings to the surface once again all the differences in outlook between the United States and the West Europeans and among the latter.

The allies have been involved in this sometimes muted but almost never-ending debate from the beginning. At first it was believed that the American nuclear monopoly sufficed to deter a conventional Soviet attack on Western Europe. After the Korean War began, the United States and to some extent the allies believed that there was a more acute threat of Soviet aggression in Europe as well as in Asia. The allies then established an integrated military structure in Europe under an American commander in chief (General Dwight D. Eisenhower was the first) and an administrative and policy structure, headed by a secretary-general. (The acronym NATO, North Atlantic Treaty Organization, is often applied to these structures and also to the alliance itself and to its military arm.) The United States built up its forces in Western Europe and called on the allies to do the same. It also insisted on a military contribution from the newly created FRG—a requirement that met strong French resistance and was agreed to only after four years of controversy.

## *Massive Retaliation*

The ambitious manpower goals adopted by the alliance during this period were never achieved. The end of the Korean War in 1953 led to a rethinking of U.S. strategy. The United States, exasperated by its prolonged involvement in Korea and reluctant to risk a repetition of such a conflict in or outside Europe, decided that it would be too expensive and too risky to try to meet Soviet or Soviet-backed aggression everywhere by conventional forces on the spot. It then developed a concept of so-called massive retaliation, which threatened a nuclear response against the Soviet homeland to Soviet aggression anywhere in any form.

The West European theater was of course affected by this shift in American policy. With the end of the Korean War and a brief stabilization of tension after the death of Soviet leader Joseph Stalin (March 1953), the allies were content to turn again to reliance on American nuclear power, which saved them some of the costs of the planned conventional buildup. But the integrated military command was maintained, and West German rearmament, which the allies agreed to in 1954, went forward. Significant U.S. forces remained in Europe, alongside sizable allied forces, as a symbol of the American commitment and a "tripwire" or trigger which, once engaged in battle by a Soviet attack of any kind, would assure the launching of a U.S. nuclear response. This assurance provided deterrence to Soviet attack.

The turn to the doctrine of massive retaliation coincided, unfortunately, with the emergence of a significant Soviet nuclear force (the Russians tested their first atomic device in 1949, their first thermonuclear device in 1953). The Soviet Union still had only a slight capability to drop nuclear bombs on the United States, but the successful launching of the first Russian Sputnik in 1957 greatly increased its prestige as a military power and foreshadowed the end of the immunity of American territory from nuclear attack. In any case, the Russians increasingly had the ability to use nuclear weapons against Western Europe. People began to argue, therefore, that the United States might not feel as free as before to meet a conventional Soviet attack with a nuclear response once the Russians could meet that with a nuclear strike on Europe, and possibly on the United States itself. The argument that the United States would not risk New York for Berlin did not emerge only in the last few years in response to U.S.–Soviet nuclear parity. It goes back more than 20 years to a time when the Russians began to have the capacity to inflict nuclear damage on the American homeland.

There was a revival of tension in the late 1950s when the Soviet government threatened to turn over its occupation rights in Berlin to the East Germans, with whom the Western allies, including the FRG, refused to have diplomatic relations. Whatever the Russians' precise intentions, their actions called up memories of the Berlin blockade of 1948-49 and fears that they and/or the East Germans might try to isolate the city from the West. If such a crisis should lead to conflict, the allies would presumably have to contemplate a nuclear strike on the Soviet Union in the absence of a capability to defend the city locally. There was more and more debate about whether that threat was a credible deterrent for the most-likely kinds of hostile Soviet actions in Europe short of massive aggression, or even for that.

*Flexible Response*

From these changes in the military balance and the debate to which they gave rise there evolved the concept of flexible response. The Kennedy Administration adopted this as the basis of U.S. military policy in 1962, and the alliance did so in 1967, after President Charles de Gaulle, who opposed the new policy, removed France from NATO's military structure (though not from the alliance itself). The purpose of this doctrine was to strengthen deterrence by broadening the range of possible alliance responses to lower-level aggression. The policy emphasized both a buildup of conventional forces and the integration of tactical nuclear weapons into alliance planning. The result, it was hoped, would be to give the alliance the capacity to manage the escalation of violence and limit it to the lowest level needed to stop a Soviet attack.

The allies (except for France) followed the American lead in shifting alliance doctrine. The logic of the flexible response policy seemed unavoidable in light of the growth of Soviet nuclear capabilities. But there was fear in Europe that the United States, increasingly vulnerable to Soviet nuclear attack, would be ever less willing to resort to strategic nuclear war for the defense of Western Europe should that become necessary. This was the beginning of the long debate about "decoupling" U.S. power from the defense of Europe. There was concern that the American desire to strengthen conventional and tactical nuclear fighting capabilities in Europe signified that the United States would no longer consider an attack on the allies as an attack on itself, to be met with the full range of its power. To the extent that the

Russians believed that, the new policies might diminish rather than strengthen deterrence.

A Soviet attack against the United States itself, inevitably nuclear, would be met by a nuclear counterstrike. But a conventional Soviet attack against Western Europe or some part of it now was to be met, according to the doctrine of flexible response, at a level appropriate to contain and defeat it. As Soviet nuclear capabilities grew over the following years, so did European concerns that the superpowers might, for their own reasons, prefer to fight a conventional or limited nuclear war in Europe while sparing themselves the costs of a nuclear exchange. The West Europeans welcomed flexible response's more realistic concept of planning to meet relatively local or low-level challenges without having to depend on a nuclear bluff that was increasingly implausible for such objectives. At the same time, they did not like the prospect that a great conventional or limited nuclear war would be fought across their territories or that the United States might let them be overrun by the Red Army with the expectation of eventually liberating them somehow, as in World War II.

This debate about the role of nuclear weapons in the defense of Europe was muted by the onset of the period of relative détente between the blocs, highlighted by the limited test-ban treaty (1963) and the Nuclear Non-Proliferation Treaty (1968), then by the four-power agreement to normalize the status of Berlin (1971), the U.S.-Soviet strategic arms and antiballistic missile treaties (1972), and the treaties by which the FRG strengthened and normalized its own relations with the Soviet Union and the countries of Eastern Europe, including the German Democratic Republic (GDR). The agenda of East-West negotiations and détente also led, after long preparations, to the opening of talks on mutual and balanced force reductions in Europe (MBFR) in 1973 and the Helsinki Conference on Security and Cooperation in Europe (CSCE) in 1975.

In this atmosphere the problems inherent in the alliance's decision to adopt flexible response were largely bypassed. In the mid-1970s, however, further progress toward détente waned and, toward the end of the decade, relations between the United States and the Soviet Union deteriorated sharply. One reason for that was Soviet activities in Africa and elsewhere, culminating in the invasion of Afghanistan in December 1979—the first time since World War II that the U.S.S.R. used its own troops to invade a country that was not one of its Warsaw Pact allies. Arms control negotiations led to a second SALT (strategic arms limitation talks) agreement that the United States did not ratify. At the same time there was a steady buildup of Soviet military capabilities that provoked increasing support in the United States for a Western response. These developments widened the longstanding differences among the allies about strategic doctrine and defense planning and revived the 1960s debate about parity and its implications for European security.

### 'Two-Track' Decision

This time the problem was made even more complex by the fact that the Soviet Union had improved its capacity to direct a nuclear strike of great accuracy against Western Europe as well as against the United States. It was argued on both sides of the ocean that Soviet preponderance in intermediate-range nuclear forces (INF) required a response in the European theater if the decoupling of the United States from Western Europe, implicit in the codification of superpower strategic parity by the SALT agreements, was not to be accentuated in the eyes of both Russians and Europeans. As a result, the alliance decided in December 1979 to modernize its theater nuclear forces by deploying 464 U.S. ground-launched cruise missiles (GLCMs) and 108 U.S. Pershing II medium-range ballistic missiles in five countries of Western Europe— Britain, the FRG, Italy, Belgium and the Netherlands—to counter the buildup of Soviet SS-20 and other accurate missiles aimed at Western Europe. At the same time, the allies offered to negotiate limits on theater nuclear forces with the Soviet Union. Such an agreement, if it could be achieved, would of course affect the number of missiles the alliance eventually would deploy, beginning in late 1983, when they first would be available. The two-track decision thus offered both a carrot and a stick to the

Soviet Union, and both a reassurance to those West Europeans who were troubled by the Soviet buildup and a hope to those who would prefer to reduce rather than increase the number of nuclear weapons—and Soviet nuclear targets—in Western Europe.

This decision in itself was not a departure from previous alliance practice. Theater nuclear weapons under U.S. control had been deployed in Western Europe for many years (there were some 7,000 in 1979). The fact that the Soviet Union objected to the planned deployments might have been expected to carry no more weight with the allies than its objections earlier to German rearmament and many other allied decisions about how to provide for their own security.

In fact, however, the alliance decision became very controversial in most of the countries in which deployment was to take place. Because the period between the decision to deploy and the beginning of deployment was four years, the sense of urgency on the allied side waned somewhat, and the Russians, in an unprecedentedly strong propaganda campaign, were able to argue that it was not their own earlier buildup which was upsetting the theater balance of nuclear forces but that planned by the alliance. Above all, international tensions increased sharply during those years. Expectations in Western Europe that SALT II would be ratified were disappointed, and along with them hopes for an agreement on European theater weapons that would obviate the need for the planned deployment, or at least reduce its scope.

As strategic and theater arms control negotiations stopped at the beginning of the Reagan Administration (to be resumed later, but without results), the opponents of deployment in Western Europe became more active in using both political weapons and street demonstrations to attempt to reverse the alliance decision. By November 1983, when deployment was to begin, Belgium and the Netherlands were still putting off their decisions about accepting the weapons assigned to them. Important groups in Italy, Britain and, above all, the FRG were challenging their governments' decision to accept deployment. To some, the new weapons seemed likely to make the deploying countries more vulnerable than before to the risk of Soviet attack without adding

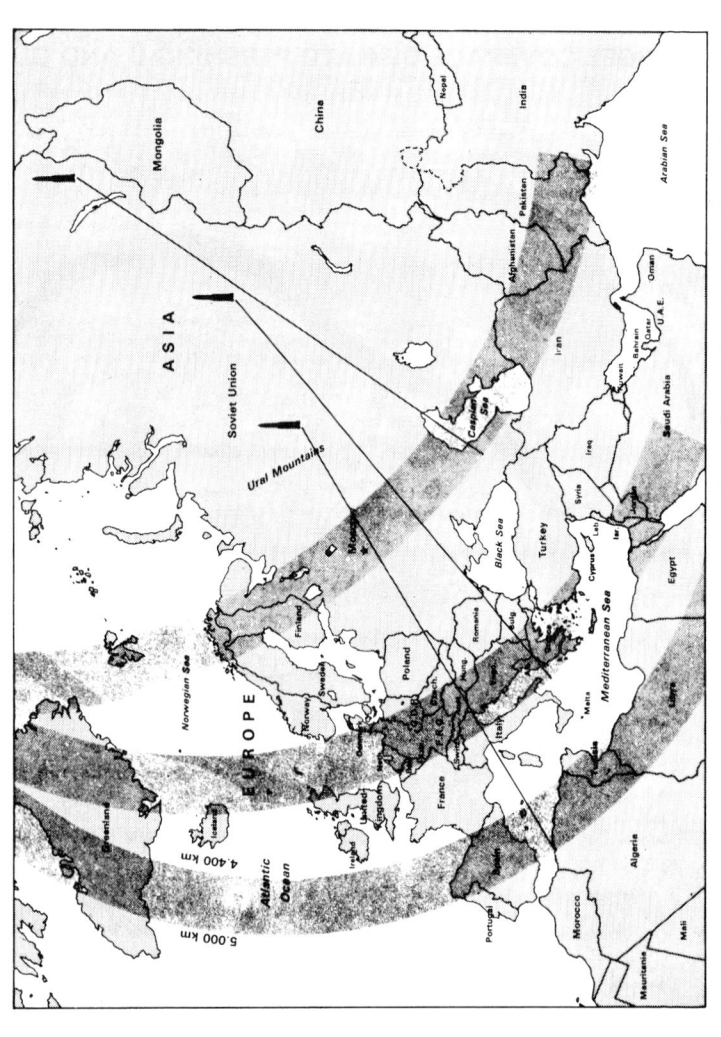

Source: NATO Information Service, Brussels, Belgium, 1984

# NATO GLCM AND PERSHING II COVERAGE

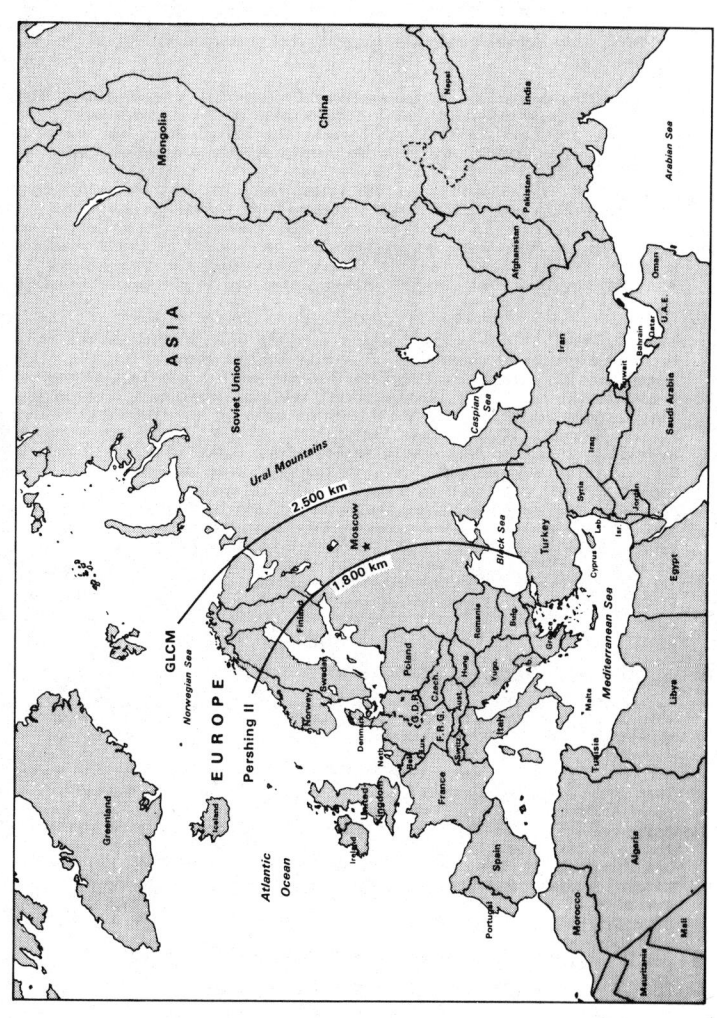

Source: NATO Information Service, Brussels, Belgium, 1984

anything to their security. Others thought deployment an unnecessary further step in an arms race that some critics blamed on both superpowers, some mainly on the United States. In the FRG the debate became linked with other themes derived from that country's particularly vulnerable position in Europe, the psychological weight of its division, its long dependence on a distant superpower for its basic security, and the emergence to voting age and even leadership of people who increasingly questioned the premises of their country's postwar policies.

### *INF and West German Politics*

The deployment debate contributed to the erosion of the coalition of the Social Democratic and Free Democratic parties (SPD and FDP, respectively), which had governed the FRG since 1969. In October 1982 the Free Democrats formed a new coalition with the Christian Democratic/Christian Social Union parties (CDU/CSU). The government headed by Chancellor Kohl was returned to office in elections held in March 1983 in which INF deployment was an explicitly posed issue, though not the only or even the main one. A new small party, the Greens, entered the Bundestag (lower house of parliament) for the first time on a platform that called for a refusal to deploy. The West German parliament voted in November to proceed with deployment, however, and it began almost at once. The issue seems of declining importance in German politics, but it continues to divide the SPD, now in opposition.

Deployment also has begun in Britain and Italy. The issue remains unsettled in Belgium, which continues to delay making a final decision. In the Netherlands, the government and parliament agreed in June 1984 to proceed with preparations for deployment but to defer it until a final decision is made in 1985 in the light of Soviet behavior with respect to further buildup of SS-20s and the results of U.S.-Soviet negotiations on the subject. Despite uncertainty about the positions of the Belgians and Dutch, the momentum of the opposition has slowed as deployment has gotten under way and the Soviet Union has withdrawn from negotiations.

The development of the INF issue in West German politics and the outcome of the intense debate provide important insights into the vulnerabilities and the strengths of the alliance in the 1980s. It is not surprising that the West Germans, situated as they are, will from time to time reexamine the international position of their country with the hope of improving it. The success of Ostpolitik (Eastern policy) from the West German point of view (discussed in the next chapter) showed that changes in relations with the East were possible and encouraged the search for further change. We can expect this in times of relative relaxation of tension but it may also occur in periods of increased tension, when the FRG feels particularly exposed to the cold blasts of superpower confrontation. What is most important about the recent reexamination is that, even with all the emotion that issues of nuclear weapons lent to it, the majority of West Germans decided, yet again, that the existing alliance system is more responsive to their needs than any feasible alternative.

But the deeper questions raised during this debate will surface again. The West German people will continue to look for improvements in their difficult and dangerous position in Europe. They want to maintain and strengthen their ties with East Germany and to shelter that relationship from the downs in U.S.-Soviet relations. Up to now, they have been able to do this while maintaining their alliance ties. But they have found no alternative to the present European system because the Soviet Union, much as it might like to draw the FRG out of the alliance, is not willing to pay the price that would be necessary if it were to have even a chance of doing so: to "release" the GDR from the Eastern bloc in order to allow its union with the FRG. The West German search is likely to resume from time to time, but the results will probably be limited and compatible with the maintenance of the alliance, until such time as Soviet control over Eastern Europe collapses. Developments in Poland since martial law was imposed in 1981 suggest that this eventuality does not provide the basis for a realistic FRG policy, and the West Germans have shown that they know it.

The debate about alliance strategy and security policy also will go on as long as the development of military technology continues. The European allies already are beginning to be concerned, for example, with the question of whether the protection of an American "star-wars" antimissile defense, if it can be developed, will be extended to them. They worry that the deployment of such a system or even research toward it will constitute further decoupling of the United States from European defense. One by-product of an arms control agreement between the superpowers to halt such developments would be to allow the alliance to fix a military strategy that would not thereafter be upset by weapons innovations. But such an agreement seems as unlikely to be achieved as Soviet collapse or German reunification.

## *Permanent Strategic Debate*

Having deployed INF missiles to deter a Soviet nuclear strike on Western Europe, the alliance now proposes to strengthen its conventional capabilities so as, among other purposes, to reduce the need for and European fears of early resort to nuclear weapons. Former ambassador George Kennan, former Secretary of Defense Robert S. McNamara, former presidential adviser McGeorge Bundy and former chief SALT negotiator Gerard Smith have proposed that the alliance build up its conventional forces substantially and consider renouncing first use of nuclear weapons in Europe. There has been little support in Europe for such a renunciation even in the midst of the INF debate. The allies fear nuclear war in Europe, but they also fear a massive conventional war on their territories. Planning for such a war seems to them to decouple further their security from that of the United States. Proposals that aim to reduce one fear aggravate the other.

The allies have been debating strategy and force levels since 1950 and continuously have advertised their disagreements on these subjects and the insufficiencies of their preparations to implement alliance plans. But the Soviet Union has never ventured to test these self-proclaimed inadequacies, even when leading analysts and statesmen have announced that nuclear parity had invalidated the American guarantee of Western

Europe. The success of a deterrent strategy should be measured, after all, by the behavior of the putative enemy. In this case the Soviet Union apparently has not been convinced by decades of allied soul-searching in public about defense to take advantage of the weaknesses so openly proclaimed to it. The present situation may, of course, be different. But the alliance and its leading members now are strengthening their defenses in significant ways. The record of 35 years gives us reason to hope that, notwithstanding internal debate, their efforts will continue to deter adventures by a hitherto prudent opponent in an area where American interests, power and prestige remain committed as nowhere else in the world.

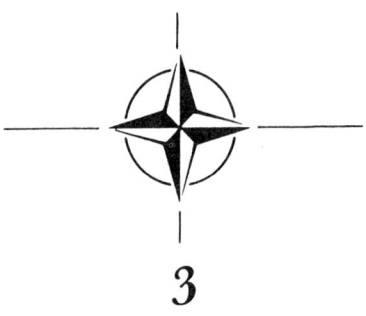

# 3

# Grand Strategy?

Traditional alliances brought together two or more countries that agreed to go to war together in certain defined circumstances but otherwise conducted their foreign affairs largely as they saw fit. The Atlantic alliance is very different. The threat it was organized to deal with has turned out to be of indefinite duration, and so has the alliance and the adherence of its members to it. The Soviet threat has become global and increasingly intertwined with developments outside the European-North American treaty area which may affect the interests of the allies. For these reasons the allies agreed in principle almost from the start that they needed to have common or at least convergent policies on much more than a defensive military strategy for Europe. What they needed, they said, was a global strategy to deal with a global threat. Many alliance statements have made this point over the years:

> Our alliance cannot therefore be concerned only with the North Atlantic area or only with military defense. It must also organize its political and economic strength on the principle of interdependence, and must take account of developments outside its own area. (December 1957)

Ministers further agreed that the stability of regions outside NATO boundaries, particularly in the South West Asia area, and the secure supply of essential commodities from this area, are of crucial importance. Therefore, the current situation has serious implications for the security of member countries. The altered strategic situation in South West Asia warrants full solidarity and the strengthening of allied cohesion as a response to the new challenges. (June 1980)

The prescription usually has been a call for enhanced consultation among the allies on the problems they faced. And, in fact, such consultation has been very extensive. Heads of government, ministers and lower-level officials of the allied countries have met regularly and often over the years, within alliance structures and outside them. In addition, there is a large military staff at Supreme Allied Headquarters near Brussels and in the subordinate commands. Consultations always can be widened and deepened further, but it cannot be said that they have been lacking among the allies.

Yet a review of alliance history makes very clear that the allies rarely if ever have had what could be called a total strategy for dealing with the Soviet Union, and even less for dealing with third-world issues which are or are alleged to be linked to Soviet policy. Consultations, particularly during crises, often reveal sharply divergent ideas about what needs to be done and even about what the problem is. There scarcely has been a year in the history of the alliance when there has not been a public disagreement among the allies.

How could such divisions among the allies be avoided? They might agree on what is to be done in every case. The record of the past and the diversity of interests, perceptions and means of action among the allies make that seem improbable even if policy consultation—on a truly give-and-take basis—was improved among them. Or, there might be an understanding that the allies would go along with whatever the United States wanted in cases when, as senior ally, it decided—ex cathedra, as it were—that the security of the West, and of the alliance, required that the members do certain things with respect to issues outside Europe.

The American government has implicitly made such a claim on certain occasions—the Arab-Israeli war of October 1973, the Soviet invasion of Afghanistan and the U.S. invasion of Grenada. But notwithstanding the preponderance of American power in the alliance and the range of its presence outside Europe, the other allies are no more likely now to accept American "hegemony" as a binding principle of the relationship than they ever were in the past.

Perhaps the most realistic prospect for improving this situation is that the allies will come to understand better both the possibilities and the limitations of their being able to agree on problems in each of the main contentious areas of policymaking. The best proof of their ability to conduct coordinated diplomacy is found in the success they had in navigating the dangerous waters of détente, from the late 1960s onward, without falling prey to that "détente fever" which some observers thought might consume the alliance altogether. The allies showed that they could concert their diplomatic actions effectively when the issues at stake—Berlin, the U.S.-Soviet nuclear arms control negotiations, and the convening of the MBFR and CSCE conferences—touched the core of alliance cooperation in Europe. Such cooperation has been maintained since with reasonable effectiveness (and much internal negotiation) in the followup meetings of the CSCE and in the various forums of arms control negotiations.

At the same time, there are wide areas in which the allies have not agreed on policies for dealing with the Soviet Union. Their differences have deep roots. U.S.-Russian official relations always were distant, and, between 1918 and 1933, nonexistent. The two countries were allies in World War II but then enemies in the cold war. For Americans, that is almost all there has been to the relationship: permanent tension or hostility tempered by some degree of cooperation at certain times and on certain issues.

For the Europeans, there always has been more to their relationship with the Soviet Union than tension. West Europeans of course recognize the implications of the division of Europe, unwelcome as these may be. But General de Gaulle expressed a widely felt view when he spoke of trying to overcome the division imposed by the superpowers and to build a new or restored Europe that would extend "from the Atlantic to the Urals." Few in Western Europe were ready to follow him along this path because he never convinced them that they could get from here to there even by taking risks (such as dismantling the alliance) which most were not ready to take. But many European leaders have also said that the political division of the Continent should not be accepted as permanent and should not be made deeper by any step they could avoid.

## *Opening to the East*

The West Germans have been particularly committed to opening doors and building bridges to East Germany since the late 1960s in line with the Brandt government's Ostpolitik of recognizing the existence of two German states in one German nation. At the height of the cold war, when the FRG was becoming a key part of the Western alignment, it insisted on trading with the GDR in order to show that it remained committed in some sense to the concept of one Germany. The later Ostpolitik provided for diplomatic relations between the two states, freer contact between their peoples, the reunification of families (mostly in the FRG) and increased trade. At the same time, the FRG also entered into treaty arrangements with the Soviet Union, Poland and others to signify that its closer ties with the GDR were not meant to challenge the Eastern bloc or Soviet interests in Eastern Europe.

The commitment of the FRG to this policy has survived the change of government in 1982. The Christian Democratic/Free Democratic coalition has maintained and expanded relations with the GDR even as it was accepting deployment of INF missiles and as U.S.-Soviet relations were deteriorating sharply. No significant group of Germans has suggested scrapping the 1972 Berlin agreement or the Eastern treaties because of that deterioration or to signal that "détente was indivisible."

This phrase was used in 1980–81 by those who thought that the Soviet invasion of Afghanistan marked a rupture in détente which should extend to all aspects of it. But even at the height of the postinvasion reaction against détente, neither the American government nor any other Western power suggested that the Berlin agreement or the Ostpolitik treaties should be cancelled. The Reagan Administration, in fact, restored the main American economic tie with the Soviet Union (grain sales) and resumed strategic and theater arms control talks. In all these areas the benefits of such ties and negotiations to the United States and/or the West presumably were judged to be at least as substantial as they were to the Soviet Union. The United States thus made clear that in practice it shared the Europeans' belief that détente, or at least its fruits, is divisible and that tension need not be made indivisible by, for example, creating a crisis over Berlin or stopping all Western trade with the Soviet Union.

## *Trade Disagreements*

Even so, there continue to be differences between the United States and some of the allies with respect to how far "normal" relations with the Soviet Union should be maintained or even extended during a period of superpower tension. This has been most evident in the area of trade. The Reagan Administration, by its recommitment to being a dependable supplier of grain to the Soviet Union, has shown that it does not want to isolate the Soviet Union altogether in the hope of inhibiting its growth or its military spending. But at the same time there is continuing U.S. criticism of the European allies for their trade ties with the East.

Overall, the trade of the European members of the alliance with the East European members of the Council for Mutual Economic Assistance (CEMA) has not been a very large part of their total trade. The allies' imports from CEMA were 3.7 percent of their total imports in 1970, 4.2 percent in 1980, and 4.5 percent in 1982 (the last year for which data is available). Their exports to CEMA were 4.0 percent, 3.9 percent and 3.3 percent of their total exports for the same years. By contrast, 0.4 percent of all U.S. imports came from CEMA in 1982 and 1.7 percent of all U.S. exports went to those countries. These data do not suggest that there is now or is likely to be overall a politically dangerous dependence on Eastern trade by the European allies. But in certain fields exports to or imports from the Soviet Union are more important to some of the allies than the overall average and conceivably might be manipulated by the Russians in a crisis.

American critics of allied trade with the Eastern bloc also argue that the deficit the Europeans are running (about $10 billion in 1982) contributes to CEMA's holdings of hard currency and thus permits the Russians to buy more and strengthen their economy in general. (U.S. grain sales have the opposite effect: they are a drain on Soviet hard currency reserves. On the other hand, by importing grain, the Russians can divert scarce domestic resources to industry and armaments.) The United States also complains that the allies on some occasions give Eastern customers preferential interest rates in order to promote exports. This question shades off from mainly economic considerations to objections of a more political or psychological nature that the allies treat the Eastern countries not only as well as they treat others but sometimes even better, which seems inconsistent with the broader obligations of alliance membership.

All the members of the alliance agree in principle to prohibit the export to the Warsaw Pact countries of items of actual or potential military application or of very advanced technology. The alliance for many years has had a Coordinating Committee (COCOM) to monitor and control such trade. In practice, there has been continual disagreement about definitions of what particular items fall under the ban. The United States has usually taken a more restrictive view of what should be embargoed than do most Europeans. The United States tends to argue that the allies are taking chances on security for the sake of profit. Europeans answer that the United States wants them to forgo sales in a futile effort to deprive the Russians of militarily innocuous items which they will develop themselves or obtain elsewhere in any case. The allies also claim that trade between the two halves of divided Europe has a positive value beyond economic benefit because it keeps open lines of contact that yet may prove important in improving overall relations between East and West, and particularly in helping Poland, Hungary and other states reduce their dependence on the Soviet Union.

*Gas Pipeline Controversy*

All these arguments came together in 1982 in the intense public quarrel between the United States and Britain, France, the FRG and Italy with respect to their decision to sell equipment to the Soviet Union for use in building the pipeline which is to transport Soviet gas for sale in Western Europe. The United States objected to the gas deal on the grounds that the allies were making themselves dangerously dependent on the Soviet Union for supply of a commodity central to the functioning of their economies. Other objections include the argument about the transfer of hard currency to the Russians, the alleged incongruity of completing such a large-scale deal in the face of Soviet-sponsored repression in Poland, and the complaint that some of the work on the pipeline in the Soviet Union was being done by political prisoners or slave labor.

The European answer was essentially that Soviet gas would amount to 25-30 percent of their gas needs but only 5-6 percent of their total energy needs and that, while they were aware of the risk of becoming dependent to some extent on the Soviet Union, the deal at least would reduce their dependence on Middle East energy sources, which already had been interrupted three times for political reasons. The Russians, they argue, have an economic interest in keeping the gas flowing and maintaining their reputation as reliable suppliers.

The issue exploded when the United States in 1982, having failed to block the gas deal by diplomacy, invoked sanctions not only against American companies planning to provide some of the pipeline equipment but also against their European subsidiaries and licensees. This action provoked the most divisive clash between the United States and its principal allies in recent years. All of the European governments denied the right of the United States to apply "extraterritorial" sanctions against companies on their soil and all refused to back out of the pipeline deal. Some of the strongest protests came from the Thatcher government in Britain, which is vigorously anti-Soviet, and the Mitterrand government in France, which has praised the American military buildup, supported the deployment of INF missiles in Europe, and reduced its diplomatic exchanges with the Soviet Union to very little. For these governments, as also for the West German and Italian, the American action represented an affront to their sovereignty and an attempt to coerce them when argument had failed.

Some observers thought for a time that there might be lasting damage to the alliance. A few months later, however, the Reagan Administration decided that the costs and risks of prolonging this quarrel were excessive. It accepted the allies' decisions on the gas deal and called off the sanctions in exchange for an agreement to study East-West trade, including exports of advanced technology to the Eastern countries.

The alliance seems to have survived this row reasonably intact, though it is difficult to weigh the cumulative negative impact of this episode, among others, on public attitudes on both sides. Perhaps the alliance even was strengthened by this unusual demonstration of unity and determination by the four main European allies. The United States, in any case, got little for its reversal of policy except a lesson: that it might be wiser in the future to judge prudently how far the allies can be coerced before, rather than after, a public exchange of angry words. Such an exchange tends to exasperate everyone and raises unnecessary doubts about the ability of the alliance to get on with its main business—providing security in Europe.

The United States, during the Nixon-Kissinger years (1969–77), had argued that economic relations with the East could be beneficial to the West to the extent that they gave the Russians an interest in curtailing their expansionism in exchange for Western help in developing their economy. The United States has since written off this policy. It has acted in recent years on the belief that cutting back economic relations with the Soviet Union will inhibit its military buildup and thus its expansionism, or slow the growth of its troubled economy, or at least send a symbolic signal that the West is disturbed about one Soviet action or another. But this approach requires that the Western countries act together if the economic deprivation is to be effective or the signal is to have maximum weight (whatever that might be). This means, in turn, that the United States has to obtain allied (and Japanese) support for its policy in given cases.

The West Europeans, however, tend to believe that Soviet foreign policy cannot be influenced significantly by either increasing or restricting economic ties. They would say that trade by definition benefits both parties and that they are not naive bargainers or any less interested in Western security than the United States. Moreover, European countries that must export on a far greater scale than the United States to live and are faced by American, Japanese and now third-world competition on world markets say they cannot afford to write off the Soviet market in the chimerical hope of changing Soviet foreign policy or to chastise the Russians symbolically for their misdeeds.

The future probably will be much like the past in these matters, probably no better and, we may hope, no worse. The United States will continue to try to persuade the European allies of the correctness of its variable views on East-West economic relations. There will be public confrontations from time to time. Up to now the U.S. government has sooner or later subordinated these issues to its broader interest in maintaining the stability and security of Western Europe in the face of Soviet power. But the issue is emotional and potentially disruptive. American opinion (including congressional) might react some day in one or another of these episodes (as it did not in the gas pipeline case) to what would seem a European propensity to let down the alliance by helping strengthen the enemy we all should be committed to containing. No American Administration ever has chosen to heat up public opinion for long. But it cannot be excluded that a future Administration might allow its own or public exasperation about such disagreements with the allies to convince it that the alliance had lost its effectiveness.

# 4

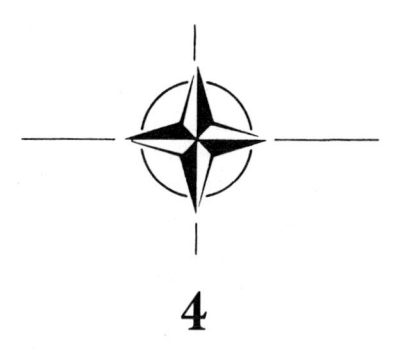

# The Third World

The North Atlantic treaty calls for the members to come to each other's aid in the event of an attack on their territories north of the Tropic of Cancer. The geographical limitation, reinforced later by the structure of the alliance's military commands, purposely excluded the Asian and African colonies of Britain, France, Belgium, the Netherlands, and Portugal. In some of these, rebellions against the colonial power already were under way. But the United States was not prepared to commit itself to help its allies shore up their colonial rule. Nor was the Soviet Union then in a position to commit direct aggression against allied possessions in Asia or Africa.

The North Korean attack on South Korea raised the question of what the allies should do about events outside Europe that affected their interests. There never has been much serious consideration of universalizing the alliance by including other non-European countries in it or by extending its protection to nonmembers elsewhere. One blind alley, pursued through the 1950s, was to construct alliances in the Middle East and Southeast Asia more or less modeled on the Atlantic alliance. But what worked in Europe, where there was a clearcut line between the two blocs and basic cohesion within the states on the Western side, was not appropriate to areas where direct Soviet aggression was unlikely, upheaval within some of the protected countries was all too likely, and important regional powers refused to join. The United States and its allies are still wrestling with the problems of how to contain Soviet expansionism outside Europe and deal with other developments outside the treaty area which affect their interests. The list of cases where the allies, or some of them, have not pursued common policies outside Europe is long.

## *Suez Crisis and its Aftermath*

Perhaps the most severe crisis the alliance ever experienced was the 1956 Suez war. The United States, angered by Egyptian President Gamal Abdel Nasser's acceptance of Soviet-bloc arms, cancelled promised aid for the building of the Aswan dam. Nasser retaliated by nationalizing the Suez Canal (controlled by a French company in which the British government was the largest shareholder). Britain and France attacked Egypt in order to regain that vital waterway and cut off at the roots what they considered the most dangerous source of Soviet-armed, third-world nationalism. The United States then sharply reversed its policy. Having denounced neutralism in general and Nasser in particular, it decided that it could not risk identifying itself entirely with the declining European colonial powers in the face of what President Sukarno of Indonesia, another practitioner of neutralism, called "the newly emerging forces." The United States then forced the ill-prepared British and French to withdraw from Egypt by refusing to help them counter an Arab oil boycott, or support their currencies, or even reassure them to their satisfaction in the face of dire warnings from Premier Nikita S. Khrushchev that the Soviet Union might fire missiles at them if they did not desist.

They did desist, with important consequences for themselves and the alliance. Britain drew the conclusion that it could not hold onto its old positions in the Middle East and Africa by force, particularly in the face of American opposition. While maintaining its independent nuclear force, it repaired its relations with the

United States. France moved in the opposite direction, fighting on in Algeria and asserting greater independence of the United States, particularly after General de Gaulle returned to power in 1958. Then, after he negotiated Algerian independence in 1962, he carried out a bold reversal of policy, making France the political or at least symbolic leader and spokesman of third-world countries trying to assert their independence of both superpowers. He vigorously criticized American policy in Indochina and urged whoever would listen in Asia, Africa, and Latin America to resist domination by either of the two "hegemonies." The fact that one of these two was his American ally gave great offense to Washington. De Gaulle's friendship with radical regimes, including Nasser's Egypt, Sukarno's Indonesia, Kwame Nkrumah's Ghana, João Goulart's Brazil and many another did not please those Americans who by the mid-1960s thought that such governments were more or less Soviet satellites or at the least hostile to the United States. How, it was asked, could France be an American ally in Europe and the friend of America's enemies elsewhere?

A new pattern of U.S.-West European disagreements about third-world developments thus emerged in the 1960s and remains broadly in place to this day. Having called on the United States to help them defend their colonial positions as part of the global struggle against communism, European governments and publics more recently have shown increasing sympathy for third-world regimes and revolutionary groups. Many Europeans see even the Marxists among these as more nationalist than pro-Soviet and are more convinced that they are entitled to pursue internal changes or revolution than is the United States, which in their eyes is the defender of entrenched regimes. The growing economic power of the developing countries, and particularly of the oil exporters, only confirms this European tendency to believe that the West should engage in dialogue rather than confrontation with these countries.

The present American Administration, on the other hand, believes that the struggle with the Soviet Union is the main focus of foreign policy and that practically every change in the developing countries can affect that struggle and, therefore, should be addressed with respect to it. The Administration believes further that, in the face of Soviet willingness to use force, threat, subversion and all other available political and economic means to advance Russian interests, the West must adapt its actions to the perceived threat in every given case. In particular, it is ready to support those abroad, whatever the deficiencies of their rule, who are resisting armed challenges by groups with direct or indirect Soviet backing.

Many Americans do not agree with this analysis, but most Administrations have acted more or less on such assumptions, limited in practice only by their conviction that the object of American support could not be "saved" (for example, the Chinese Nationalists in 1949 or the shah of Iran in 1979) or by the unwillingness of Congress and the public to provide the means thought necessary (for example, Indochina in 1975).

## *European Perspective*

Some West Europeans share the official American outlook. But a majority probably do not. It sometimes is said that American and West European policies diverge because of differences of interest. But that usually is not the case. West Europeans do not want to see Soviet influence spread in the third world any more than Americans do. Nor is the difference rooted in West Europeans' blindness to the plain facts. They understand very well the implications for themselves of, for example, a cutoff of Persian Gulf oil.

Except for France and Britain, the European allies lack military means to influence events in the developing countries. They therefore tend to minimize the importance, or doubt the feasibility, of using such means. Further, having gone through the traumas of decolonization since 1945, Europeans are more inclined than many Americans to believe that upheavals in the third world are inevitable and not likely to be stopped by anything the West can do, but also that the outcomes can be lived with.

The West Europeans do not perceive all third-world regimes and their enemies as necessarily friend or foe. They are not certain, for example, that regimes and groups calling themselves

Marxist or receiving Soviet aid are now, or necessarily will be in the future, Soviet dependencies.

On the one hand, therefore, many West Europeans think that the West can do no more to save threatened regimes than it did for Chiang Kai-shek's China or King Farouk I's Egypt or Hashemite Iraq. On the other hand, they note that these very countries, at first thought to be hopelessly pro-Soviet and anti-Western under their new regimes, in fact eventually improved their relations with the West to an at least tolerable level. The Russians, they think, can be useful in helping revolutionary groups to power but are not very well endowed with the means to help them improve their economies. In addition, the developing world is full of local quarrels (as, for example, that between Ethiopia and Somalia) in which West and East can support one or another side (and can be used by both) without clearcut ideological distinctions or definitive power-bloc alignments between the local contending parties.

West Europeans ask whether it is worth the cost and risk to try to save threatened friends who cannot save themselves and, in any case, may be replaced by regimes which are not necessarily so anti-Western as to jeopardize major Western interests. Only a few third-world countries really have the means—because of their size, resources, influence, or geographical situation—to threaten important Western interests. West Europeans are therefore less inclined than Americans to take seriously, least of all for symbolic reasons, the "loss" of small or remote countries or to believe in domino theories. Nor have they believed—as is sometimes alleged in this country—that the validity or credibility of the American guarantee to European security hinged on continued U.S. support for some beleaguered third-world friend. They think that Western Europe is uniquely important to the United States, that the U.S. commitment to them has nothing in common with its involvements with third-world countries in upheaval, and that the Soviet Union knows this.

Fortunately for the alliance things are somewhat better in practice than these differences in principle would suggest. The United States itself is not as rigid in applying the containment policy to third-world conflicts as its official rhetoric might suggest. Nor are the Europeans uniformly critical of U.S. activities in the developing countries. They can be actively supportive in cases where they judge that their own interests are involved. The French government, the most outspokenly critical of American policies in the third world, has been perfectly willing to work with the United States, or parallel to it, in the interventions in Shaba (1978), Lebanon (1982) and Chad (1983). The British and Italians as well as the Americans and the French took part in the multilateral force in Lebanon.

In other cases the West European allies have been willing to acquiesce in American military actions after a certain amount of criticism, when these are (as in Grenada) quick and successful. The French also have been willing to pull their punches in some instances (as in Central America) when the problem in question was not at the forefront of world attention and when, in addition, they had other reasons not to differ too persistently with the United States.

*Iran and Afghanistan*

Even so, U.S.-West European divergences on these issues can be profoundly divisive, as we saw in 1980 during the Iranian and Afghanistan crises. American belief that these situations called for enhanced Western military preparation and economic sanctions did not inspire much support in Western Europe. Some Americans thought this reflected blindness to imminent dangers. The West European answer, had the matter ever been discussed in a straightforward way, probably would have been that, first, the Soviet Union had gone into Afghanistan not in order to prepare a direct attack on, or even subversion of, the next tier of states but to preserve a tottering "fraternal" regime; second, the Russians were not likely to invade Pakistan or Iran even in the absence of a credible Western plan to fight them there; third, such a fight with the U.S.S.R. in such places could not be won; and fourth, the West could not save the shah of Iran or most other regimes in the area from their internal enemies by force and should not make a bad situation worse by trying to do so. Rather, it should plan to make the best deal it could with the next rulers, whether of the fundamentalist right or the radical left, on the basis of their continuing interest in selling oil and buying Western goods and technology.

For these reasons the West Europeans were skeptical about the effectiveness of economic sanctions against either Iran or the Soviet Union. Most of them were even reluctant to bother with the symbolic sanction of withdrawing from the Moscow Olympic games.

The West European prescription for such cases, which might seem to be to do nothing and wait for the dust to settle, is a difficult one for the United States to accept in cases where it thinks its prestige and/or more specific interests are deeply committed. This is particularly true when it thinks that Western action might be able to affect developments. But things are no better when the United States, convinced that it cannot just do nothing, has trouble finding an effective course of action. In the alliance crisis of 1980, the United States, frustrated by its inability to do as much about either Iran or Afghanistan as the situation seemed to require, felt obliged to take what steps it could. The success of these steps, such as it might be, depended in many cases on the support of the allies. In the absence of as much support as Americans thought they should receive (and there was some), they blamed the allies for the lack of success. The allies, in turn, found American policy not only futile but dangerous because it might lead to conflict or at least, as discussed in the previous chapter, to a widening of tensions.

In an ideal world the United States and the European allies would talk these differences through (if not out) and find where they were able to achieve common policies in the third world and where, in the absence of agreement, they at least could mute their criticisms of each other. Also, they might rethink their habit of pledging solidarity in conference communiqués that haunt them when the promised solidarity fails to materialize in the next crisis.

Unfortunately, it is not likely that the allies will do any of these things. There will continue to be clashes between them with respect to third-world issues. These, in turn, will put new difficulties in the way of the main business of the alliance: providing security in the North Atlantic area.

To limit these risks, the West European allies should consider carefully how they might play a more constructive role in situations which, as in the Middle East, affect them deeply. Their record of aid and their involvement in trade with these regions, in addition to innumerable other ties, provide an important basis on which they can build. Then they might be able to influence American policy better, as they wish, and avoid being left to carp at the most active ally.

The United States no doubt will continue to be far more involved than the West Europeans in political and military upheavals in developing countries. On it falls the main burden of acting when action is indicated, but also of determining with prudence whether Western and American interests are in fact at stake in given challenges. West European views of these matters are not uninformed and should be listened to before American policy is decided upon.

When, however, the United States decides to take action which some of the allies will not back effectively, and sometimes not even verbally, it must also decide to what extent it should try to invoke alliance solidarity in Western Europe in order to obtain West European cooperation elsewhere. The ploy does not always work, because the allies believe that the United States maintains the alliance in Western Europe for reasons of its own national interest and not for love of them, and that they owe it cooperation in Western Europe but not obedience there or elsewhere. That happens to be the case, but Americans, including the American government, do not always remember it. They should make a special effort to do so whenever they are tempted to threaten the West Europeans with dire consequences for the alliance if the allies fail to support one or another U.S. policy elsewhere.

No Administration has ever tried to implement such a threat, which therefore has always been no more than bluff, or even simply spleen. But a succession of such episodes has placed strains on public support for the alliance on both sides of the Atlantic. As long as security cooperation in Western Europe remains important to all the member countries, their leaders should wish to limit the number and divisiveness of such clashes with respect to cooperation elsewhere. Perhaps the best rule is that the West European allies should do more and the United States should expect less.

# 5

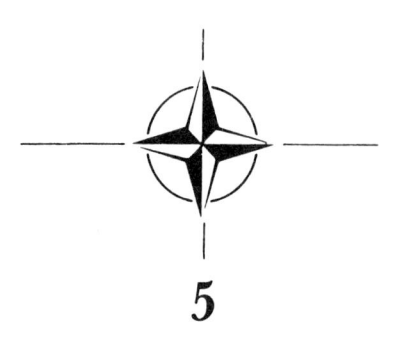

# Economic Relations

During the 1980s, economic problems have been as great a worry to every member of the alliance as they ever have been. But we hear much less talk now than we did from the mid-1960s to the late 1970s that such problems could become so serious as to erode alliance cooperation. This is due in part to the reemergence of security concerns and a tightening of alliance bonds. But we have also learned from the experience of those earlier years that the allies are able to insulate their security and political cooperation from their economic quarrels. The lessons learned help explain why the latter did not override the former even in the period of détente and are not likely to do so either in present tension or future relative relaxation of tension.

The years before the first energy crisis of 1973–74 were a period of growth and prosperity for the countries of Western Europe as well as the United States and Japan. But the very success of the postwar international economic system gave rise to new relationships among the major participants which challenged the system itself. By the early 1960s the continental European countries had achieved unprecedented levels of growth, productivity and output. Their currencies were strong. They played a central role in world trade. Their economic dependence on the United States had ended. Six of them, including the three most important, were working to spur growth and strengthen their collective weight in the global economy by joining together in the European Economic Community (EEC) or Common Market. This new state of affairs became evident as the American balance-of-payments deficit increased during the 1960s and the dollar, which had replaced the pound sterling as the main instrument of international trade, came under pressure.

The alliance as such played little part in the development of these issues but was affected by the growing friction between its principal member and most of the others. The allies have proclaimed almost from the start that their ability to cooperate successfully in dealing with the Soviet threat in Europe required cooperation also with respect to economic policy. For a time some suggested that the alliance itself should take on economic functions. But this was unnecessary because the leading countries in the alliance were also those which (together with Japan) dominated the International Monetary Fund (IMF), the International Bank for Reconstruction and Development (the World Bank), the General Agreement on Tariffs and Trade (GATT), the Organization for Economic Cooperation and Development (OECD), and other international economic institutions. Presumably they could resolve their economic differences in these existing forums—if they could resolve them at all. In addition, the West European allies preferred to manage their economic relations with the United States in places where its great economic strength was not reinforced further by its security leadership.

## *The 'Nixon-Connally Shock'*

These differences were contained during a series of monetary crises and trade quarrels in the 1960s, but nothing seemed to work for long. In August 1971 the United States suddenly and unilaterally "solved" the American problem—from its point of view. President Richard M. Nixon and Treasury Secretary John B. Connally decided to end the convertibility of dollars into gold, which had led to continual speculation against the dollar, and imposed a surcharge on existing tariff rates. This had the effect of curtailing European and Japanese exports to the United States and so forcing the exporting countries to negotiate a revision of exchange rates in a crisis atmosphere favorable to American interests.

The European allies and Japan were outraged at the abruptness and scope of what was called the Nixon-Connally shock. Coming as it did at a moment when East-West tension was relatively low, this unilateral American action on an issue of major importance to the well-being of all the countries involved, accompanied by official American rhetoric that blamed foreigners for U.S. economic problems, provoked one of the most serious crises ever among the allies. The effect on U.S.-Japanese relations was equally negative. Some predicted that the shock might make further security cooperation impossible between the United States and all its allies, European and Asian.

This did not turn out to be the case, however. The American action was followed by hard bargaining which ended in December 1971 with a realignment of exchange rates, including a devaluation of the dollar, to the advantage of U.S. exports. After further monetary perturbations, the leading countries agreed in March 1973 to let their currencies float within certain limits. The monetary system drawn up at Bretton Woods, N.H., in 1944 was shattered and has never been replaced, except by supposedly temporary arrangements which, for better or for worse, had to carry the capitalist countries through the even more severe economic storms that began soon after.

### *Global Economic Crisis*

No sooner were the problems of 1971–73 adjusted than the Western countries had to face the first energy crisis, arising out of the 1973 Middle East war, and the problems of accommodating to sharply higher energy costs. Inflation and recession followed. The second oil crisis in 1979 provoked even higher energy costs and inflation, then a full-fledged global recession more serious than any since the 1930s, with low growth and high unemployment everywhere. Recovery now is under way, but it is not clear how it will affect each of the advanced countries, and for how long.

The difficulties of the Atlantic governments have been increased by the fact that the unprecedented integration of the global economy has made each country even more vulnerable than before to the problems of the others. In addition, just at this time a new challenge has arisen: the increasing competition offered to the older industrialized countries on world markets by newly industrializing countries of the third world. Whole industries in Western Europe and the United States are threatened. The march of advanced technology toward what has been called a third industrial revolution has been more rapid in the United States and Japan than in Europe. High levels of employment and social welfare programs that have been taken for granted in Western Europe for decades are under challenge.

The mechanisms of international economic policymaking and policy coordination have not succumbed, but they have not responded very innovatively either. One new institution invented in 1975, the economic summit, brings together every year the chiefs of state or government of the United States, Britain, France, the FRG, Italy, Japan and Canada to consider the state of the world economy. These meetings have kept the leaders in touch with each other's problems, but the record of the summits, preoccupied as they often are with noneconomic events of the moment, has not been lustrous.

Nor have these years of crisis been the finest hour of the Common Market. On the contrary, there have been increasingly serious quarrels within the European Communities about the division of costs and benefits. These debates seem to have stifled whatever impetus for greater unity might have been expected to emerge in response to the clear need for Western Europe to defend its interests in a very troubled world economy. The innovation of electing the European Parliament by direct vote in the member countries so far has had little impact. France and the FRG, however, with some other countries have managed to keep their currencies linked in the European Monetary System (EMS) as a means of protecting their very important trade relations.

In these circumstances it is not surprising that there has been an increase in protectionism everywhere. What is surprising is that up to now it has not been more extensive. Apparently most governments believe that they do not dare move too far down that path because their countries are now too deeply and irreversibly tied to the global economic system to allow them to run the risks of retaliation.

Most of the European governments have criticized U.S. economic policy sharply for "exporting" inflation or recession or both. They have argued that high U.S. interest rates were attracting the world's capital to the disadvantage of everyone else's growth and were crippling the ability of third-world countries to invest, trade and meet their debts, thus further slowing the recovery of European countries more dependent than the United States on third-world markets. The French Socialist government even hinted at one point that it might try to link its alliance role with changes in U.S policy with respect to, for example, interest rates. But neither France nor any other country has acted in this way. The recession has not allowed most members (except the United States since 1981) to increase or even maintain their levels of defense spending. But the allies have again been able, as in 1971–73, to shelter their security ties from their economic differences.

In addition, the record of these years of crisis suggests that the economic ties that bind together the members of the global capitalist or free-market system, in bad times as well as good, are stronger than one might expect considering the competition among them, and among the private economic actors and the multinational companies that operate in them. There have been predictions since the first energy crisis that the industrial countries would compete more and more intensively for raw materials, for markets in which to make the money they need to pay for their energy and other imports, and for investment capital. Many thought that the old dollar-centered trade and monetary systems, reconstituted de facto in 1971–73, would not survive the shocks that followed and would be replaced by a movement toward greater national or regional economic self-sufficiency, with the larger countries resorting more and more to protectionism and monetary controls. Some foresaw the emergence of a more decentralized monetary system based on the Japanese yen and a European currency unit as well as the dollar.

## *Unity in Adversity*

These things have not happened. The unity of the free-world economic system has been maintained to an extraordinary degree, considering the successive shocks to which it has been subject since 1973. This should not be so surprising, after all. The keystone of capitalism is competition, among private economic actors as well as among countries. The latter can compete for sources of supply and markets while at the same time remaining united in defense of the overall system within which they are operating. The United States and its European allies, competitive as they may be in economic practice and divided as they may be in economic policy, have shown that they have a common preference for shoring up the overall economic system rather than trying to replace it with regional or national alternatives. Some of them (the French Socialist government, for example) may have come to this choice because, by themselves, they can neither change the system nor function outside it. All of them might like to put the system into better working order. But whatever their motives, they have shown considerable skill in keeping the system going in very difficult circumstances. In addition, new economic actors— including the Organization of Petroleum Exporting Countries (OPEC), industrializing third-world countries and also some East European countries—have been taking their places in the broad system, which has not been disrupted by their arrival but has adapted itself to make room for them.

This is not to say that the present system as managed by the leading countries in the 1980s has not exacted heavy costs from them, including lost production, high unemployment and the social and political ills that these bring. Also, improvisation can be expensive. The acute problem, raised in 1973–74, of how the industrial countries and many countries in the third world would meet their higher oil bills was resolved by "recycling." The sellers of oil invested their proceeds in other countries through the international banking system, which in turn lent the money to those in need. This, of course, created another problem now on the international agenda: repayment by countries that borrowed more than they can repay, or even service, in a period of international recession and high interest rates. New devices are being constructed to deal with that. Perhaps this system of improvisation will come to an end with a big bang. But that is not at all certain. International capitalism has found ways to keep the participating countries afloat during a severe recession. The ingenuity of the system should not be underestimated.

The record of these very difficult years gives some reason to believe that if the allies are able to deal adequately with what may continue to be severe economic problems, they should also be able to shelter their security cooperation in the alliance from their economic divisions. One question that we cannot answer with confidence, however, is whether years of hard times may not have a lasting negative impact, more severe than any we have seen so far, on the political institutions and the social cohesion of some countries. If they do, then we might expect that the "new politics" that may arise in one country or another could have unforeseeable effects not only on its economic behavior but on its international policies as well. But that has not happened anywhere in the last difficult years, and it may not happen at all if the current recovery takes hold and is maintained.

# 6

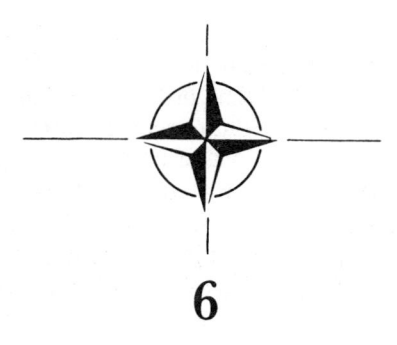

# The Future

The Atlantic alliance has done its main job well for more than 35 years. None of the member countries has been attacked by the Soviet Union or forced to accept its ultimatums by threat of attack. The line of division in Europe remains essentially where it was in 1949 (the few changes, with respect to Finland and Austria, have been favorable to the West). The countries of Western Europe have maintained their free societies and achieved previously undreamed of economic growth. The Federal Republic of Germany has gained a secure and respected place in Western Europe in a way that has won the assent of most West Germans as well as of their European neighbors. The United States has been able to build and maintain a position of strength in an area which, because of its population, wealth, productivity, influence, and location, still occupies an essential place in any American policy which aims to maintain a global balance of power with the Soviet Union.

At the same time, the Soviet Union has not mellowed or collapsed, nor has Western Europe become strong and united enough to provide for its own security without an American guarantee. Few informed people expect either of these things to happen soon. Does this mean that the Atlantic alliance is likely to survive indefinitely? It probably does, provided that the members continue to have a realistic view of the global balance of power and of their own interests. That, of course, cannot be guaranteed. The fact that Americans and West Europeans for two generations or more have on the whole pursued sensible policies in Europe provides no assurance that they will continue to do so. The very success of the alliance in helping to maintain stability in the North Atlantic area over so many years has led some people to overlook the causes and take the results as self-generating and self-perpetuating. They are not. But even those who believe the alliance can and should be maintained know that the allies have been almost constantly divided by a large number of issues and wonder whether such divisions will not sooner or later disrupt their ability to cooperate on security. The allies are no more likely than in the past to agree fully on the many problems before them. Their divisions may be even more dangerous in the years ahead because security, political and economic issues, all serious in themselves, are becoming more numerous and more simultaneous.

Wisdom and good judgment are not, of course, necessarily distributed among the members of the alliance in the same proportions as power. The asymmetrical relationship between the United States and the other allies can breed an overconfident presumption of leadership on one side, a frustrated and sometimes embittered sense of dependence on the other. Many Americans and West Europeans have hoped since the early 1950s that this disparity of power could be reduced or even overcome if the major West European countries would unite. A "United States of Europe" would have the population and productive capacity to play a much more important role in European and world affairs than even the strongest West European state can do now. But no such "Europe" has emerged, notwithstanding three decades of effort to move toward it.

### *'European Caucus'*

Various groupings of European countries have jointly developed certain items of military equipment, but neither the WEU

Bas, *Tachydromos,* Greece

nor any other body really fills the role of a European caucus within the alliance. A number of leaders recently have urged that the WEU be reactivated to allow the allies to develop common approaches to alliance issues and perhaps common programs for dealing with them. The United States has every reason to encourage greater West European self-reliance and self-confidence with respect to defense, particularly if that means a buildup of European conventional capabilities. But a few speeches or meetings do not assure success in a field which has been strewn with disappointments.

The American government, which at times had seemed more "pro-European" than the Europeans, wisely decided in the late 1960s that the pace of European unity could be set only by the participating countries. Only their desire to play a stronger role in the world, and to achieve a more nearly equal position with the United States in the alliance, could induce them to overcome deeply rooted attachments to their ancient nationalisms. But that has not happened. Innumerable episodes of West European exasperation with American policies and resentment of American "hegemony" have not led them to take actions that might make a difference. Apparently the West European allies prefer to maintain their sovereignties and national structures, even at the cost of having to rely on a distant superpower for their security, rather than give them up in the hope—which perhaps they do not believe in—of ending that dependence.

Both the British and French nuclear forces are being strengthened, and there are suggestions from time to time, as there have been since the early 1970s, that they might be coordinated in some way so as to supplement or in part replace West European reliance on the American guarantee. But coordination of nuclear forces presupposes a common decisionmaking authority with common foreign policies if the forces are to have deterrent credibility. In other words, a "government" is required. But there will be no British-French government in our time. Each country supports its independent nuclear force because it is independent. Further, the British force is linked to the United States in ways which undermine its independent credibility, at least in the eyes of continental Europeans. The Mitterrand government, for its part, has said that the strengthened French nuclear force cannot be expected to protect others. Mitterrand has told the West Germans to look to the alliance and the United States for their security.

*A New Structure?*

Revamping the structures of the alliance to increase West European contributions to it or confidence in it are equally unpromising prospects. A larger West European conventional input to the alliance would be a good thing but would not in itself change the fundamental relations between the member that provides a nuclear guarantee and the others. The naming of a West European as commander in chief, as suggested by former Secretary of State Henry A. Kissinger, has little support in Western Europe and would do little in existing circumstances to convince the Europeans that they were more nearly the masters of their fate than before. Such a step might well have the opposite effect insofar as it would remove one of the most visible links between West European security and American nuclear power, an American general in charge of the one with direct access, through his unique relationship with the President of the United

States, to the other. No West European could fill that essential bill, nor could an American deputy to a European commander in chief.

The West Europeans, furthermore, would find it difficult to agree on the nationality of a European commander. A West German would seem indicated, but there are difficulties in the way of that which might be raised not only by the FRG's Western neighbors but by those in the East. We may ask whether the FRG itself would welcome this promotion. France is not a participant in the alliance's integrated military system. The other West European countries have only relatively small forces on the Continent. Naming a general from a small country to head the allied forces is not the same thing as naming a statesman from such a country to be secretary-general. A degradation of the effectiveness of the supreme command—which, in the hands of an American, plays a political as well as military role—would seem the most likely outcome.

## *Burden-Sharing*

Many Americans hope that the allies will assume a larger part of the defense burden in Western Europe now that the United States is increasing its strategic and extra-alliance military capabilities. The issue of burden-sharing has been one of the most permanently vexatious in alliance history. It seems manifestly unfair that the United States should spend 6.6 percent of its gross national product on defense (1983) while Britain spends 5.5, France 4.2, the FRG 3.4, and the other allies (with the exception of Portugal, Greece, and Turkey) even less.

The allies are aware of the importance of the problem for American opinion. They know that many Americans, including many members of Congress, believe that the Western European countries are rich and populous enough to provide a larger share of the conventional means of defense needed to protect Western Europe. Moreover, their peoples would seem to have an interest in providing the alliance with the conventional means that would allow it to delay or possibly avoid the use of nuclear weapons in an eventual conflict.

Some of the West European allies, at least, may increase their spending once economic recovery takes hold. But there are reasons that help explain, if not justify, why the allies are not likely ever to spend as large a share of their income on defense as the United States does. The United States is not only by far the richest country in the world but pursues a policy of global containment of Soviet expansionism. The costs of that policy are enormous, involving a full panoply of nuclear and conventional forces. The largest West European states do not think in those terms. They have global interests and insights but not global means of action that can be compared in any way to those of the United States. The fact that they themselves were once global powers in an older sense of the term confuses more Americans than it does Europeans about the possible present role of the European countries. In theory there is no reason why a European country that spends 4 or 5 percent on defense could not spend 1 or 2 percent more. In practice, however, another scale of measurement is at work. Rich and less rich families do not spend the same proportion of their income on housing, food, entertainment, diamonds, and investments. The European countries are not poor, but they do not see the world, and their role in it, with the same eyes that the United States sees its own position.

## *The United States and Europe*

All this may seem discouraging to Americans who find, in the 36th year of the Atlantic alliance, that there is little prospect that their burdens in Western Europe can be reduced soon in response to either a change in Soviet policy or some fundamental shifting of roles and responsibilities between the United States and the West European allies. American policymakers, Congress and the public all might wish for better—as they might also in other parts of the world—but, in the here and now, they have to make and support policy for Western Europe as it is. That is what the United States has done since the 1940s. The result has been decades of debate among the allies, undoubted American costs and risks related to the U.S. presence in Europe, and the equally undoubted fact that a part of the world essential to any policy of global commitment has been made secure, stable and peaceful, and kept free, as almost no other.

There is, of course, a recurrent tendency in the United States to have done with Europe. The country was founded, after all, in an act of revolution against the old world and its ways. America's destiny lay westward. The fact that the West European allies often seem so uncooperative in things that matter to the United States, and even in their own defense, does not make it easier to maintain steady American participation in an alliance system that seems to many unnatural.

In the end the United States is, as always, the most important variable in the survival and success of the Atlantic alliance. For as long as the United States believes it must maintain a global balance of power with the Soviet Union, it will have to take account of the local balance in Europe. This does not mean a "choice" of Europe over other areas—a global power can sustain a global policy if necessary—but a recognition of the self-evident fact that, while Europe is no longer the center of the world, it is still a uniquely important part of it. There may be theoretical alternatives to the Atlantic alliance that would secure American interests in the stability and independence of Western Europe at less cost or risk. But none seems feasible notwithstanding years of search on both sides of the ocean. The United States and the West European allies together seem bound by the facts of international life to make the best of a relationship which, with all of its flaws and exasperations, has for 35 years served them not perfectly but well.

# Talking It Over
*A Note for Students and Discussion Groups*

This issue of the HEADLINE SERIES, like its predecessors, is published for every serious reader, specialized or not, who takes an interest in the subject. Many of our readers will be in classrooms, seminars or community discussion groups. Particularly with them in mind, we present below some discussion questions—suggested as a starting point only—and references for further reading.

## Discussion Questions

Why was the Atlantic alliance formed in 1949? What did its founders expect it to accomplish?

In what ways has the alliance met their expectations? In what ways has it failed to meet them?

Why has the alliance survived for 35 years? What has been its main accomplishment? What other things has it done?

In the 1950s the alliance adopted a strategy of massive retaliation, in the 1960s a strategy of flexible response. What was the objective of each? Why did the second strategy replace the first?

Why did the alliance decide in 1979 to deploy intermediate-range nuclear missiles in Europe? Why did this give rise to controversy? What has it shown about the strengths and weaknesses of the alliance?

In what cases have the allies been able to work together effectively in their dealings with the Soviet Union? Why have they been unable to do so in other instances?

Explain the differences between the Reagan Administration and the European allies with respect to trade with Eastern Europe.

Why have the allies found it so difficult to work together in the face of Soviet expansionism and other changes in the third world?

Why does the author say that the Suez war of 1956, the "Nixon-Connally shock" of 1971 and the Iran and Afghanistan crises of 1979–80 were perhaps the most divisive episodes the alliance has experienced?

The allies have had many disagreements about trade and monetary affairs over the years. What effect have these had on the alliance?

The author is skeptical about the prospects for much increased West European defense cooperation or basic change in the structure of the alliance. Do you agree or disagree with him?

The author suggests that the alliance will go on indefinitely. Why does he think so? Do you agree?

## READING LIST

Barnet, Richard J., *The Alliance—America, Europe and Japan: a History of the Postwar World.* New York, Simon and Schuster, 1983.

Bertram, Christoph, "The Implications of Theater Nuclear Weapons in Europe." *Foreign Affairs,* Winter 1981/82.

Bundy, McGeorge, Kennan, George F., McNamara, Robert S., and Smith, Gerard, "Nuclear Weapons and the Atlantic Alliance." *Foreign Affairs,* Spring 1982.

DePorte, A. W., *Europe Between the Superpowers: The Enduring Balance.* New Haven, Conn., Yale University Press, 1979.

———, "Europe and the Superpower Balance." HEADLINE SERIES 247, New York, Foreign Policy Association, December 1979. (An abbreviated version of the above book).

Flynn, Gregory, and others, *The Internal Fabric of Western Security.* Totowa, N.J., Allanheld, Osmun, 1981.

Grosser, Alfred, *The Western Alliance: European-American Relations Since 1945.* New York, Continuum, 1980.

Joffe, Joseph, "Europe's American Pacifier." *Foreign Policy* No. 54, Spring 1984.

Kaiser, Karl, and others, "Nuclear Weapons and the Preservation of Peace." *Foreign Affairs*, Summer 1982.

Rogers, General Bernard W., "The Atlantic Alliance: Prescriptions for a Difficult Decade." *Foreign Affairs*, Summer 1982.

Sloan, Stanley R., and Gray, Robert C., "Nuclear Strategy and Arms Control." HEADLINE SERIES 261, New York, Foreign Policy Association, November/December 1982.

Tucker, Robert W., and Wrigley, Linda, eds., *The Atlantic Alliance and Its Critics.* New York, Praeger, 1983.